Butterflies

American Museum of Natural History

A Book of Postcards

Pomegranate

SAN FRANCISCO

Pomegranate Communications, Inc.
Box 6099
Rohnert Park, CA 94927
www.pomegranate.com

Pomegranate Europe Ltd.
Fullbridge House, Fullbridge
Maldon, Essex CM9 4LE
England

ISBN 0-7649-0709-3
Pomegranate Catalog No. A522

Text by Eric L. Quinter,
Department of Entomology,
American Museum of Natural History

Pomegranate publishes books of
postcards on a wide range of subjects.
Please write to the publisher for more information.

Designed by Shannon Lemme
Printed in Korea
07 06 05 04 03 02 01 00 99 98   10 9 8 7 6 5 4 3 2 1

To facilitate detachment of the postcards from this book, fold each card along its perforation line before tearing.

The butterfly prints in this book represent the work of Edward Donovan and John Obadiah Westwood and are from the rare book collection of the American Museum of Natural History.

Edward Donovan (1768–1837), an artist and naturalist, published works on natural history illustrated with his own exquisite and accurate watercolor paintings. He also founded the London Museum and Institute of Natural History in 1807.

In 1798, Donovan published *An epitome of the natural history of the insects of China: comprising figures and descriptions of upwards of one hundred new, singular, and beautiful species; together with some that are of importance in medicine, domestic economy, &c. The figures are accurately drawn, engraved, and coloured, from specimens of the insects; the descriptions are arranged according to the system of Linnaeus; with references to the writings of Fabricius, and other systematic authors.* The book was more encompassing than Donovan imagined or intended—for it includes paintings and descriptions of insects as far removed from China as Africa and South America. The specimens which Donovan illustrated were from the cabinets of contemporary collectors and were frequently of dubious provenance. In 1800, Donovan published a larger volume on India in the same style as the earlier work.

Donovan faithfully attempted to match his purported Chinese butterflies with botanical backgrounds featuring Chinese plants drawn from examples growing in London gardens. This attempt to lend authenticity was unfortunately far off the mark. Many of the butterflies shown here are not naturally attracted to any flowers, but instead have a fondness for fermenting sap, decaying fruit, or even less appealing substances.

John Obadiah Westwood (1805–1893) was an entomologist and accomplished archaeologist who was gifted with a rare artistic talent. As an entomologist, he was unrivaled in his day. He developed multiple specializations across the field and prepared numerous monographs complete with accurate illustrations, the scope of which would put modern entomologists to shame. He was also a prolific writer on natural history. His *Introduction to the Modern Classification of Insects* was published in two volumes in 1839 and 1840, and instantly became the best textbook in English on entomology, remaining so throughout the nineteenth and into the twentieth century.

Westwood was elected Fellow of the Linnaean Society in 1827 and was a founding member of the Entomological Society of London in 1833, where he later served as Secretary and President. In 1855 he received the Royal Medal of the Royal Society. In 1858, Westwood became the first Hope Professor, Chair of Invertebrate Zoology, at Oxford—a position he held for the remainder of his long life.

In 1842 Westwood published a revised edition of Donovan's 1800 work on India in which Donovan's engravings were painted by Westwood. In 1848, Westwood published his own work executed in Donovan's style, *The cabinet of oriental entomology; being a selection of some of the rarer and more beautiful species of insects, natives of India and the adjacent islands, the greater portion of which are now for the first time described and figured.*

LEPIDOPTERA.

: Papilio . Agenor :

: Papilio . Crino .

London Published as the Act directs by E.Donovan June 1798.

Butterflies

Edward Donovan (English, 1768–1837)
Upper: *Pachliopta coon* Fabricius
110 mm wingspan. Assam to Java
Lower: *Papilio memmon agenor* Linnaeus
130 mm wingspan. Widespread throughout SE Asia

Pomegranate   BOX 6099, ROHNERT PARK, CA 94927

American Museum of Natural History
©AMNH

LEPIDOPTERA.

Papilio Laomedon.

London Published as the Act directs by E. Donovan april 1 1796.

Butterflies

Edward Donovan (English, 1768–1837)
Papilio protenor Cramer
110 mm wingspan. China

Pomegranate BOX 6099, ROHNERT PARK, CA 94927

American Museum of Natural History

LEPIDOPTERA.

Papilio Glaucippe.   *Papilio Sesia*

London, Published as the Act directs by R. Thornton, November 1798.

Butterflies

Edward Donovan (English, 1768–1837)
Upper: *Ixias pyrene sesia* Fabricius
45 mm wingspan. Southern and western India
Lower: *Hebomoia glaucippe* Linnaeus
90 mm wingspan. India, Nepal, to Myanmar (Burma), China,
Thailand, Cambodia, and Malaysia

BOX 6099, ROHNERT PARK, CA 94927

Pomegranate

LEPIDOPTERA.

* *Papilio Pyranthe.*   * *Papilio Phila.*

London, Published as the Act directs by T.Ehrenreen Jan.r 1 1798.

Butterflies

Edward Donovan (English, 1768–1837)
Upper: *Catopsilia pyranthe* Linnaeus
50 mm wingspan. Throughout SE Asia
Lower: *Phoebis philea* Johansson
70 mm wingspan. Southern U.S., Mexico, Central
and South America

BOX 6099, ROHNERT PARK, CA 94927

Pomegranate

LEPIDOPTERA.

Papilio Oenone. *Papilio Almana.*

Papilio Laomedia. *Papilio Salentina.* war

London Published as the Act directs by I.Donovan 1817-1-1798.

Butterflies

Edward Donovan (English, 1768–1837)
Upper left: *Junonia hierta* Fabricius
50 mm wingspan. India and Sri Lanka to China
Upper right: undetermined nymphalid butterfly, ventral view
ca. 50 mm wingspan. Range unknown
Lower: *Junonia almana* Linnaeus
50 mm wingspan. Throughout SE Asia

Pomegranate BOX 6099, ROHNERT PARK, CA 94927

LEPIDOPTERA

Papilio Priamus.

London, Published as the Act directs, by Zimmerman, Feb.y 1, 1800.

Butterflies

Edward Donovan (English, 1768–1837)
Ornithoptera priamus priamus Linnaeus
130 mm wingspan. Serang, Ambon, and lesser
Indo-Pacific islands

Pomegranate   BOX 6099, ROHNERT PARK, CA 94927

American Museum of Natural History
©AMNH

LEPIDOPTERA.

Papilio Parthous.

London, Published as the Act directs by E.Donovan. January 1.1800.

Butterflies

Edward Donovan (English, 1768–1837)
Troides hypolitus Cramer
140 mm wingspan. Celebes

Pomegranate BOX 6099, ROHNERT PARK, CA 94927

American Museum of Natural History

LEPIDOPTERA.

Papilio Ulysses.

London, Published as the Act directs by J. Sowerby, Mead Place.

Butterflies

Edward Donovan (English, 1768–1837)
Papilio ulysses Linnaeus
110 mm wingspan. New Guinea to Ambon

Pomegranate   BOX 6099, ROHNERT PARK, CA 94927

American Museum of Natural History

LEPIDOPTERA.

* *Papilio Lethe.* * *Papilio Cresses.* *
* * *Papilio Torridata.*

London, Published as the Act directs by E.Donovan, March 1 1805.

Butterflies

Edward Donovan (English, 1768–1837)
Upper right: *Cyrestis cocles* Fabricius
50 mm wingspan. Myanmar (Burma) to Malaysia
Middle left: *Hypanartia lethe* Fabricius
50 mm wingspan. Southern U.S. and Central America
to Brazil and northern Argentina
Lower: *Charaxes tiridates* Cramer
90 mm wingspan. Sierra Leone, Ivory Coast,
Nigeria, Ghana, and Democratic Republic of the Congo (Zaire)

BOX 6099, ROHNERT PARK, CA 94927

Pomegranate

LEPIDOPTERA.

Papilio. Phegea. **Fatima. Thyelia.**

London. Published as the Act directs by J. Zimmerman. May 4. 1800.

Butterflies

Edward Donovan (English, 1768–1837)
Upper: *Elimniopsis phegea* Fabricius
75 mm wingspan. Liberia to Gabon
Middle: *Anartia fatima* Fabricius
50 mm wingspan. Mexico to Panama
Lower: *Symphaedra nais* Forster
60 mm wingspan. India

Pomegranate BOX 6099, ROHNERT PARK, CA 94927

1. Papilio Antenor.   2. Papilio Antilipus.

Butterflies

Edward Donovan (English, 1768–1837)
Upper: *Pachliopta aristolochiae* Fabricius
80 mm wingspan. Widespread throughout SE Asia
Lower: *Atrophaneura (Pharmacophagus) antenor* Drury
120 mm wingspan. Madagascar

BOX 6099, ROHNERT PARK, CA 94927

Pomegranate

1. Oxatheptra Heliacon. 2. Papilio Silans

Butterflies

Edward Donovan (English, 1768–1837)
Upper: *Papilio anchisiades idaeus* Fabricius
90 mm wingspan. Mexico to northern South America
Lower: *Troides helena* Linnaeus
110 mm wingspan. Widespread throughout SE Asia

BOX 6099, ROHNERT PARK, CA 94927

Pomegranate

2. *Papilio Astyanax.*   1. *Papilio Polymnestor.*

Butterflies

Edward Donovan (English, 1768–1837)
Upper: *Papilio polytes* Linnaeus
90 mm wingspan. Nepal and India to Java
Lower: *Papilio polymnestor* Cramer
120 mm wingspan. Southern India and Sri Lanka

BOX 6099, ROHNERT PARK, CA 94927

Pomegranate

1. *Vanessa Cacta.*   2. *Nymphalis Octavius*
3. *Nymphalis Athamas.*

Butterflies

Edward Donovan (English, 1768–1837)
Upper left: *Polyura athamas* Drury
50 mm wingspan. India and Ceylon to southern
China and Malaysia
Middle: *Salamis cacta* Fabricius
60 mm wingspan. Sierra Leone to Democratic Republic
of the Congo (Zaire) and Ethiopia
Lower left: Memphis species, undetermined
ca. 70 mm wingspan. Central or South America

BOX 6099, ROHNERT PARK, CA 94927

Pomegranate

1. *Nymphalis Hipponæ* 2. *Ithonia Cyane.*
3. *Nymphalis Cyanite.*

Butterflies

Edward Donovan (English, 1768–1837)
Upper: *Consul fabius* Cramer
90 mm wingspan. Mexico, Central and South America
Lower left: *Cethosia cyane* Drury
75 mm wingspan. India, Burma, Thailand, and Malaysia
Lower right: *Neptis coenobita* Stoll (?)
ca. 60 mm wingspan. Eurasia

Pomegranate

BOX 6099, ROHNERT PARK, CA 94927

Butterflies

John Obadiah Westwood (1805–1893)
Figure 1 OR Figures 1, 2, 3, and 5: *Atrophaneura polyeuctes*
Doubleday
115 mm wingspan. India, Nepal, Tibet, Bhutan, and southern China
Figures 2–5 OR Figure 4 (upper left) only: *Atrophaneura*
dasarada Moore
110 mm wingspan. India, Nepal, southern China

BOX 6099, ROHNERT PARK, CA 94927

Pomegranate

Butterflies

John Obadiah Westwood (1805–1893)
Ornithoptera priamus poseidon Doubleday (male)
130 mm wingspan. West Irian and Papua New Guinea

Pomegranate BOX 6099, ROHNERT PARK, CA 94927

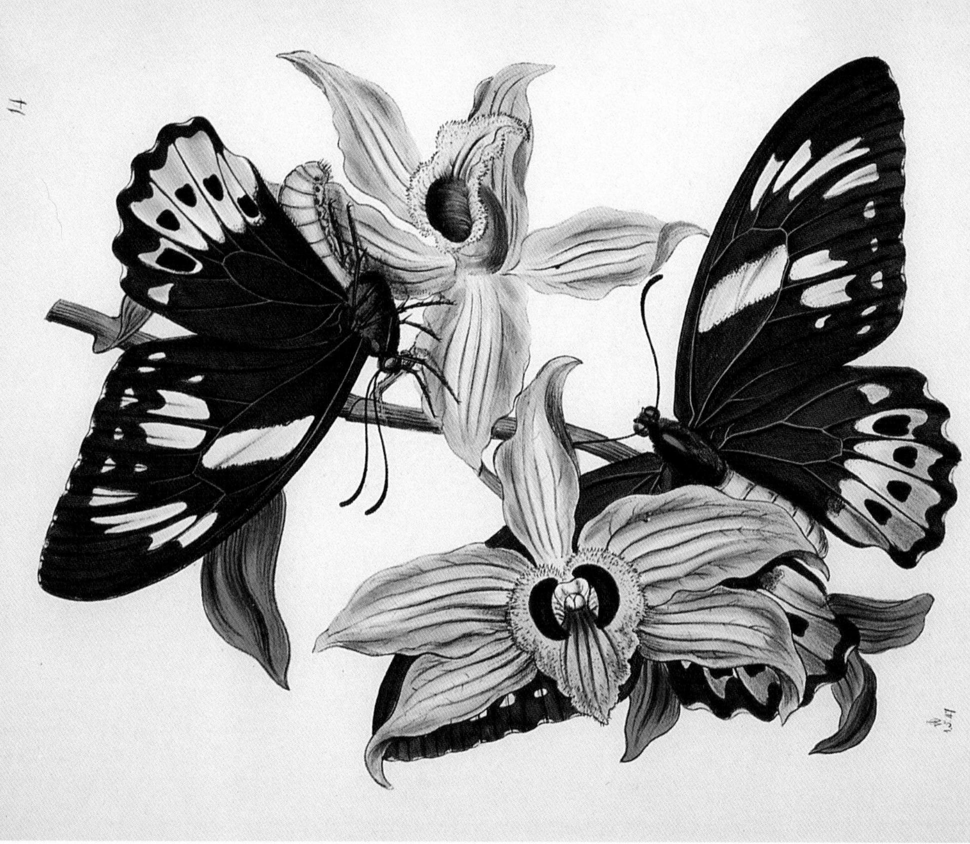

Butterflies

John Obadiah Westwood (1805–1893)
Ornithoptera priamus poseidon Doubleday (female)
150 mm wingspan. West Irian and Papua New Guinea

Pomegranate

BOX 6099, ROHNERT PARK, CA 94927

American Museum of Natural History
©AMNH

Butterflies

John Obadiah Westwood (1805–1893)
Figures 1 and 2: *Amathuxidia amythaon* Doubleday (male)
100 mm wingspan. Sikkim, Assam, and Myanmar (Burma)
Figure 3: *Amathuxidia amythaon* Doubleday (female)
100 mm wingspan. Sikkim, Assam, and Myanmar (Burma)
Figure 4: *Amathusia phidippus* Linnaeus
90 mm wingspan. Myanmar (Burma) to Java, Bali, and Philippines

BOX 6099, ROHNERT PARK, CA 94927

Pomegranate

21.

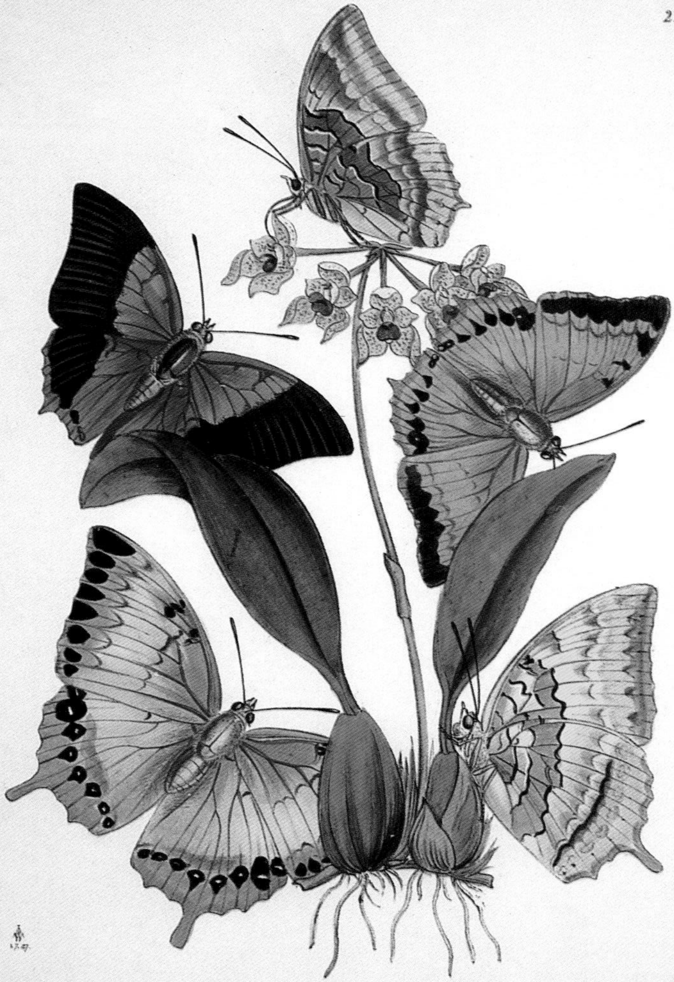

Butterflies

John Obadiah Westwood (1805–1893)
Upper left and top: *Charaxes psaphon* Westwood
70 mm wingspan. Sri Lanka
Upper right, lower left, lower right: *Charaxes marmax*
Westwood
70 mm wingspan. Sikkim, Assam, Myanmar (Burma),
Vietnam to Malaysia

BOX 6099, ROHNERT PARK, CA 94927

Pomegranate

American Museum of Natural History
©AMNH

Butterflies

John Obadiah Westwood (1805–1893)
Upper and lower left: *Polyura dolon* Westwood
70 mm wingspan. Northwestern India and Nepal
Upper right: unidentified nymphalid butterfly
130 mm wingspan. "Assam"
Lower right: *Kallima philarchus* Westwood
80 mm wingspan. Sri Lanka

Butterflies

John Obadiah Westwood (1805–1893)
Upper left and right: *Papilio elephenor* Doubleday
100 mm wingspan. Assam and western Myanmar (Burma)
Lower left and right: *Meandrusa payeni evan* Doubleday
110 mm wingspan. Sikkim to southern Myanmar (Burma)

BOX 6099, ROHNERT PARK, CA 94927

Pomegranate

American Museum of Natural History
©AMNH

Butterflies

John Obadiah Westwood (1805–1893)
Upper left: *Euploea algea deione* Westwood
90 mm wingspan. Sikkim to northern Myanmar (Burma)
Upper right: *Idea hypermnestra hypermnestra* Westwood
140 mm wingspan. Borneo
Lower left: *Idea hypermnestra belia* Westwood
140 mm wingspan. Java
Lower right: *Neurosigma siva* Westwood
85 mm wingspan. Sikkim, Bhutan, and Assam

BOX 6099, ROHNERT PARK, CA 94927

Pomegranate